Faith
Death
and
Randomness

By
km pierce

Faith Death and Randomness

Copyright 2006 by km pierce (Saeligstone)

All rights reserved. No portion of this book may by reproduced in any form whatsoever without the written permission of the author.

ISBN: 978-0-6151-5985-0

Published by km pierce (Saeligstone)
www.saeligstone.com

First Printing, February 2006

Table of Content

Faith (Untitled 1)	**3**
Promise	4
Artist	5
Damascus	6
Water Walkers	7
Time	9
The Children	10
The Meal	11
The Seeds	12
Lord, We Drown!	13
Reborn	14
Death (Untitled 2)	**15**
Last Laugh	16
Tell Me	17
Live Burial (Over Your Grave)	18
Ashes to Ashes	19
Life is a Dream	20
Little Boy	21
Snow White	22
Dream	23
Randomness (Untitled 3)	**25**
Purple Night	26
Cold Shoulder	27
Goodbye, Friend	28
Am I?	30
Voices	31
Moon Sister	32

Table of Content

Cheers	33
Lost	34
Mind Racing	36
Not Anymore (Channeling Poe)	37
Hidden	39
You	40
Spectacle	41
Blush	42
Aphrodite's Joke	43
Alive	44
Vikings	45
Infinity	46
The Picture	47
Chimera	49
Time	50
Decipher	51
Melt	52

Faith

Honey covered lemon drops
Fall from forehead to page
Slide out of mouth -
Evaporate on air…
This is the only way to catch them.
Strong, meek, sweet
All a code
Colors and fragrances
My brain…
Staining the snow

                                             -Untitled 1

Promise

Critical conditions at best;
Heart lost as depressed you confess
Sins against Me

Tribulation made you worry
Made life blurry as you scurry
Through streets of broken dreams
Trying to make a buck -

What luck!
As it's all taken from you
And you're stuck with just Me, again…

I'm by your side all you need to stay alive.
The world - everything is against you
Deception, destruction - intention to kill you
Come back - I'll fill you
Follow Me - I'll heal you
Love Me as those against Me harm you
You are Mine.
I won't leave you

Artist

God is an artist.

He molded life from clay
And painted the living canvas
Where we work and live and play

God is an artist.

He filled the world with sound
The whispering summer breeze
Birds and crickets chirping
Crunchy autumn leaves

God is an artist.

He writes the story of every life
From humans to insects small
With love and hope and fear and strife –

God is an artist.

And if we listen carefully
To the earth's spinning core
We'll find the answers and questions
To life and death and more

God is an artist.

Damascus

On a mission, on a road
Now it's different than before

A great light caused us
To fall on our knees
What is this? Who is this?
Tell me please!

It was He that I'd persecuted
I saw the truth, the light
Just a moment before
It all became night

I sat in darkness for three days
The scales fell away and I could see
Who I was and what I'd had done

Against these precious followers of the Son
Yet they took me in…
And soon called me friend,
Brother,
Apostle,
Paul

Water Walkers

He was always the most rash
Of all of them
Brother Peter jumped out of the boat
To greet Me
On the water

My heart felt light at that moment
He looked to Me and was unafraid

Then I was dismayed,
He had come so far
And now I watch him sinking
Flailing his limbs as his body
Fell below

I caught his hand

I pulled him up
Patted his shoulder
He laughed sheepishly
Embarrassed, then awed
As he saw how far he'd walked
From our fishing boat

The others were silent
And watching...
Their brother, My student
Our Father's human son

"Tripped a bit..." He muttered
To no one in particular
"You didn't stay focused on Me." I said sternly.
"I never said I did it with my feet."
He grinned.

I smiled, also
And then we walked
Back to our boat again

Time

Time is slowing down
The scientist's say
Things aren't so quick
As in Adam's day
Life moves more quickly
But time more slowly
Is that why we don't live
Ancient – as in those olden days of glory

The Children

We had rebuked them
And He us…

Now I stand
Watching as they approach Him
Some shyly looking up into His face
Others rambunctious – climbing, wrestling
He doesn't put them in their place.

They dance and sing and play
He delights in their games
And I suddenly learn a lesson –
This is how to praise God:
Living, loving, jumping, running,
Spinning, examining, chasing, squealing, laughing…
This is why He loves us.

And how we should show our love for Him
By forever being like these
Beautiful, little children

The Meal

"We can't send them away like this."
Jesus said as we began to dismiss the crowd.
"They must be fed." He said.
"With what, Lord,
"Shall You turn stone to bread?"

He gives me a peculiar look.

A small boy walks forward
He holds up a small lunch for us to see
"I want to share."

Five loaves and two fishes
And a child's simple wishes

Some of the crowd hears and snickers
But the Lord thanks the child
And the people sit and wait.

And 5,000 are fed because of the kindness of a child
And the power of our Lord

The Seeds

The children made necklaces
A bouquet of flowers - one for each of us
The Lord made such fuss over their little gifts.

We wore them for days and weeks
A month in all –
Then they began to fall from around our necks
And, standing near a barren field
Jesus said, "Let us bury them down here.
"And when I am gone away, if you are afraid,
"Come here and think on this day."

Then suddenly He was gone
First dead, then alive, now away up in Heaven
And we are persecuted on every side
I am afraid.

And I sit here and think how those few tiny seeds
Have become this great sea of flowers

Lord, We Drown!

Running about
Storm clouds
Mist and water
Boat rocking
Death knocking
Don't you hear, Lord?

We'll all go overboard.

The sturdy boat
A fragile toy -
Unruly child's hand
We stagger, stand,
Stagger again…
Trying to steady our place

Lord, wake up! Make haste!

His eyes flutter open
He rebukes our fears
He stands and faces the storm
"Stop," He says.
And all is quiet.

He goes back to bed.

REBORN

Jagged edge of lightening
Flashing, blinding
God's power – frightening –
Wind picking up
Gonna be a storm
Gonna break it up
Smash it all apart
Start again

Rain falls, sand to mud
Mud to clay, no where to hide
All night, no day
Pray and hope the earth
Doesn't swallow

Rocks move, with screech and groans
Earthquakes, hot lava flows
A nuclear break

Fire erupts

People sizzle in the rain

The earth is reborn

DEATH

Shafts of light shine down
A sun hidden behind clouds
Dark and mysterious; fluff and play

The scraggly and gnarled limbs of the tree
Are the hands and arms of a thousand dead
Reaching forever toward the heavens
Aware now of hellish dread

-Untitled 2

Last Laugh

Life isn't lived it's used
Often abused
A user's last hit
Smooth walled pit
Elevator of loss

Is this it?

Being born we learn
Yet have no one to teach
To each his own errors
Repeats of the ones
Former generations made

All the same lies
Different phrases, that's all
For similar reasons
From different faces tears fall

Shattered dreams realized
Too late
Mock for what should have been
Should have done
Past
As it ends you remember
It's Death's last laugh

Tell me

What would you do if I died tomorrow?
Will you be okay?
What would you do if I ended sorrow -
This tragic, comic play

What would you do if I died tomorrow?
Will you visit my grave?
What would you do if I ended sorrow –
In this cold and lonely place

What would you do if I died tomorrow?
Would you care, anyway?
What would you do if I ended sorrow -
In some ordinary way

Tell me what would you do?
Would you think of me at all?
Would I be a memory forgotten?
Some sad unknown and lonely girl –

That's all?

Live Burial
(Over Your Grave)

Live in a grave
Claw in a coffin
Screaming weaker
Needing oxygen
Hope
Someone
Will
Wall
Over
You

Ashes to Ashes

Carved down to the bone
Passion just a stone
A watery grave –
There's nothing here
Or in between
Nothing close or far
To be seen
Nothing new and nothing old
Only death our fate unfolds

Life is hell, living damnation
For what was I ever given creation?
No purpose at all
No drop of hope
A bloody stain
Deserving all - endless pain
Everything's lost, broken and cold
I know I am nothing – mold upon mold

Life is a Dream

Between ocean and ocean
She dreamed of life
Breathing - last breath
Killed by death
Medicines she needed
Not brought to her bed

Between there and home
He dreams of life
Taken - tiny metal domes
Sent by death
Like hot through butter
Ripped open chest

Life is a dream
Only some get to attempt
Honor those who lost their chance
Force yourself to succeed

Little Boy

Broken walls and the blackened sky
The skin of my friend is hanging
Hanging...
Dried in the wind

No one speaks and no one cries
Dissolving heat before my eyes
Their throats are dry...
Dried in the wind

And I don't think about market street anymore
And I start to wonder if we will win this war
I wonder and wonder and wonder some more
Where is my little young one?
Dried up, dried in the wind

The fire encased me all around
And there is nothing but death in my town
The heat from the blast bubbled the ground
There was a loud sudden rushing sound --
But now, we're dried and forgotten...
Dried in the poisonous wind

Snow White

Heart bleeds, soon I'll die
Life forgotten, soul to fly
Far, far away

I live in fear
I've not lived at all
And
One day soon I will fall into the arms of death

And no one will remember me...
And no one will place what's left of me
In a coffin of glass for all to see

Dream

There is a place with silver lakes
Where purple flowers bloom
And life's ashes, pains and aches
Are left behind in gloom…
A place where extra is ordinary
We can walk upon the moon
Swim deep in roaring oceans
After hiking the sun at noon

There is a place where winter's grace
Clean snow upon the ground
Melts not at all forever
Hushing every sound
Another, yet, where autumn's touch
Paints the lands and sky
Golden, red, and orange
As the rushing wind sighs

There is a place with blue-green seas
Hot sand that's crystal white
And caverns deep with secrets
Spicy days and warm clear nights
A final place with verdant land
Splashed with flowery hues
Where silken breeze and sunny kiss
And gentle rain falling, soothes.

There is a place between sky and earth
Where all these lands survive
We can go there anytime
We just have to close our eyes
But listen close and carefully
To the danger therein be
It's easy to lose the self
If endless dreams we weave

So hear the call and wake up
Dwell in reality
Lose hope, wish, and sleep…
Never dream of being free
For dreaming is a deadly thing
Veiled and thinly disguised
A reaper grim, with grinning face
And ghastly glowing eyes

RANDOMNESS

I saw a leaf suspended
Hung by a clear-thin rainbow rope
Refracting light as the wind battered
Twirling, spiraling...
Dancing a jig
Beyond its control

It wasn't frightened
Nor stressed
It hung there, swinging in the wind
Laughing at power
Its autumn brown color
Sparkling in the light

-Untitled 3

Purple Night

Acquaintances mist away,
And friendships melt into the purple night
Never to be renewed.

So, the world becomes lonely
Without embrace or friendly face
Void… sleep… stone…
There's nothing to feel anymore
No peace, pain, ecstasy -- I avoid
Closed -- not unhappy --

It's the best I can hope for
I think all I deserve, perhaps
I'm not good enough.
Not smart enough.
Not pretty enough.
Too broken to be made whole
Though it's kind of you to try
Within you, I've glimpsed the true blue of day
Always out of reach

Cold Shoulder

The indifferent ice
I feel
Is the price
You heal
My wounds with
My mind
Gone unreal
Lost in white
A mist

Colors all around me
Turned
Green to black
The life you found me
A shadow
There's no looking back

The indifferent ice
I feel
Is the price
You heal
My wounds with
Life
A spinning wheel
A jaded, ancient myth

Goodbye, Friend

It wasn't you that broke me,
That happened years ago.
A hundred-thousand fears
And tears ago
I stopped.

No more...

I quit.
It's been easy, I'll admit,
To fade away into darkness
The solace of loneliness
The enjoyable nothingness –

The almost peacefulness...

But now,
It's all mixed up.
Confusion, dissolution
Sadness
Gladness

Pain...

I have no protection
My breath
My suffocation
My inspiration
My rest

My friend,
I'm afraid…

This should end.

AM I?

Am I still home to you?
Once you told me so
Long before you left
A lifetime ago

Am I still home to you?
A place to rest and think -
Or has that feeling gone away
In a second's blink?

Am I still home to you?
I wonder sitting here, alone,
You've avoided my presence -
Dug-up human bones

Voices

A thousand voices
Shout inside my head
Each trying to get out
Onto paper

A thousand voices
Clamor for attention
Hoping to be the one
I'll favor

These thousand voices
Speak to me
Fragmented piece of mind
Scattered across
A lonely sea
Fathoms of space and time

These thousand voices
(Once might have mattered)
Are now only
Broken thoughts
And dreams
Shattered

Moon Sister

The moon calls me
Sister
Far into the night
Follow, wander,
Discover
What I've missed
What I've lost
What I need to find
Life

The moon calls me
Sister
Changing every night
Kind; kind of
Sinister
Death and love
Hope and hate
Need and want
Unite

Cheers

Serpentine words twist
My pen sings as mind soars
Sore hand struggles to keep up
The happy side
Laughing like a hyena
With festering meat, gorging...
Sweltering sun – a carcass –
Someone else's kill

Lost

Daddy's little boy grew up
Daddy didn't know
Daddy's little boy grew tough
Daddy wasn't home

Snatched food from a tiny mouth
Whiskey more to hold
Little boy's health went south
For whiskey he was sold

Daddy's little boy grew up
Daddy wasn't home
Daddy's little boy needs love
Daddy had no soul

People paid - took boy in
Made him earn his gold
Lent him out to older men
To fill his feeding bowl

Daddy's little boy grew up
Daddy had no soul
Daddy's little boy lost trust
Daddy died of cold

Ran away from master's house
Fast as he could go
Spraying bullets brought him down
Left dying in a hole

Daddy's little boy grew up
Daddy died of cold
Daddy's little boy died rough
Daddy didn't know

Mind Racing

I think about everything
Nothing at all
Let me watch where I step
Let me watch where I fall

Suspicious of happy
More friendly with sad
Comprehend I am peace-less
Understand I am mad

Fade away for a while
My mind – a sea
Doing much, a little bit
Discovering me

Not Anymore
(Channeling Poe)

Astronomers are fastened by outer space
Musicians hear the tune-filled core
Of the place where we live
Things we're searching for

I am none of these and nothing.
I am not anymore.

Writer's write legends and truths
Thespians our reflections explore
We listen to them carefully
Debate their lies, lives and more
We listen to them carefully
Read and watch with every pore

I am none of these and nothing.
I am not anymore.

Lawyers make lies veracity
Doctors cure and fine
Their prices are never cheap
But we use them all the time
We listen to them carefully
And pay their hefty fines
To find the things we're searching for
We pay really hefty fines

I am none of these and nothing.
I am not anymore.

There are others out there
Many others who do and think
Who feel and rest and live
Add to complex happenings

But I

I am none of these and nothing.
I am not anymore.

Hidden

It clears the head
The poet thing
It seems easy
To rhyme and sing

The past is past
The future's gone
All at last
This present fun

Is where I think
And rest inside
I linger here
And hide and hide

You

Chasing rabbits
Four or five – not just one
Testing limitations
You climb always for the sun

What happens when you reach it?
And your rabbit stew is done?

I guess that's the intrigue –
That's the game of the thing.
How close can you get to almost catch?
How far before blistering?

Most folks prefer turtles to rabbits
And cool oceans instead of the sun.
But from you we can learn a good habit,
Never quite until it's done.

Spectacle

I am a rabbit
Chased down a hole
The fox is after me
My heart pounds

I am a rat
Caught in a trap
Wounded not yet dead
Chewing through my arm
To escape human hand

I stand wrapped in cellophane
Suffocating, surrounded by air
While people pass,
Ignoring
And others sit and stare

Blush

O! Forget I spoke a single word!
Put that notion from your head!
It was just a jest you thought you heard,
Not something that I really said.

Forget I said those five small words
Seven syllables, curiously thread –
Me? Ask so bold? Absurd!
So worry not and laugh instead.

Forget! Forget! Forget those words...
Spoken out of fear that fled
Disjointed as a fallen bird...
Smashed on the ground – crystal lead

Aphrodite's Joke

Laughing
Aphrodite's joke
Cupid at her side
Tripped over your smile
Shuddered when you sighed

Mock of human condition
Crushed through lack of volition
Explanation:
The ancients needed amusement

Love's latest ambition
Practicum in misery
I can't object
Built walls no longer protect
This bloody hears yours -
Collect

Keep it safe and warm

Alive

Nothing makes you feel so alive
As looking death in the eyes
And laughing into that grim face
Staying secure in this place
The world is full of strange and dangerous –
It's true,
But how you react is up to you
Hide away self-prison safe
Or get out and explore this place
We call
Earth

Vikings

Lightening flashes
Over burning ashes
Pillagers' cloud –
They took
And shook
Forsook
And look!

They've gone away...

We will rebuild our lives.

Infinity

One mirror in front of another
I stand in the middle
Staring before and behind
Facing eternity
Seeing the future and past at once
I feel strange and lost
Afraid, hopeless
And small
As I stare in the mirrors tall
I miss the present moments, today

The Picture

Paint me a picture
Red, blue, and green
Create for me a simple scene.
"Blue is the sea,
Red hot sun in the sky,
And green is the place that I like to lie
And watch little ants go by."

Paint me a picture
White, black, and grey
Tell me about this place and day.
"White is the snow,
Grey the bark on the trees,
Black, full clouds go tumbling by
Rumbling through the sky."

Paint me a picture
Of your life –
"This world full of pain and strife?
Where daddy hits and mommy cries?
Oh, please, oh, please let me paint the sky
And the pretty world that's going by."

Goodness

"I can't make you happy." He said to me.
"Only you can do that. So go, be free."

(Lovely like a bird – that is me.)

But I've fallen, tumbled down
I'm broken, stomped into the ground
I've no wings – that is me

(Broken little bird – that is me.)

"Wings or not – walk and run.
Eventually you'll find the fun.
You know you are the only one
Who can set you free." He said to me.

Chimera

Pale and dark – a fusion
Two become one
I am my brother
I am my sister
Male? Female?
Neither, both
Either

Time

Tick-tock
The world spins slowly
Time slows down as we speed up
Moving faster and faster than ever before
One day soon we'll hit the floor
Exhaustion – gasping
We'll beg for rest
But that word will be lost.

Decipher

Echoes inside my mind
Stop me
Stop time
Make me question land and sky
Echoes inside my mind

Frequency in outer-space
Bring hope
Bring faith
Of another living world place
Frequency in outer-space

The song of the whale intrigues me
The tune of the heavens frightens me
I wonder what it's for
What are they trying to say?

Melt

The straight lines and even circles around me
Must melt into chaotic theory
An ordinary person's hell

I never want to forget the past
Remember you and me?
The future's something I hope will last
Until the last night that I be

www.ingramcontent.com/pod-product-compliance
Lightning Source LLC
Chambersburg PA
CBHW031432040426
42444CB00006B/768